Skills for Internal Consultants

Participant's Coursebook

by

Penny L. Ittner
Donald G. Roberts
Alex F. Douds

Copyright © 1999, HRD Press, Inc.

All rights reserved. Any reproduction of this material in any media without written permission of the publisher is a violation of United States copyright law.

Published by: HRD Press, Inc.
 22 Amherst Road
 Amherst, MA 01002
 800-822-2801 (U.S. and Canada)
 413-253-3488
 413-253-3490 (fax)
 http://www.hrdpress.com

ISBN # 0-87425-514-7

Acknowledgements

We would like to acknowledge the many people who helped to make this training product a reality.

First, we would like to thank Peter Block for his consulting skills model, first published in his book, *Flawless Consulting: A Guide to Getting Your Expertise Used*, back in 1981. As consultants, we have been guided by his model and his approach. As teachers, we have used his model as a framework for teaching others the art and craft of consulting. We especially appreciate his permission to use his model in the creation of this workshop.

Next, we would like to thank our colleagues—the internal and external consultants with whom we have worked—who have unselfishly shared their ideas and their talents to help us succeed in our consulting projects and grow as consultants.

Finally, we would like to thank the clients with whom we have worked over the years. Their trust in us to help them solve important problems or seize significant business opportunities has given us the experience and confidence in the collaborative consulting process upon which this workshop is based.

Penny L. Ittner
Donald G. Roberts
Alex F. Douds

About the Authors

Penny Ittner has spent the past 20 years as a human resource/organization development consultant, helping clients in both the private and public sectors achieve their organizational goals. Prior to establishing her own training and consulting business in 1984, Penny spent eight years as an internal consultant for the Bell System. During divestiture of the Bell System, she worked with AT&T executives and their teams, helping them make successful transitions from the traditionally regulated environment of the Bell System to the highly competitive, international telecommunications environment of today. As an external consultant, Penny's clients have included such organizations as Air Products and Chemicals, Inc., Bell Atlantic, GTE, BDM, AES, the U.S. Department of Agriculture, the U.S. Department of Health and Human Services, and the Federal Judicial Center. Penny holds a degree in Business Administration and an M.S. degree in Human Resource Management from Johns Hopkins University in Baltimore, Maryland. She currently serves as adjunct faculty member at Marymount University in Arlington, Virginia, where she teaches consulting in its Graduate School of Business.

Don Roberts spent the last 30 years as a human resource/organization development practitioner, consultant, author, and educator in the U.S., Southeast Asia, and Australia. He was one of the first internal organizational development (OD) consultants in the telecommunications industry, establishing a comprehensive internal OD group that grew to over 50 members serving C&P Telephone, a company of over 40,000 employees. In 1982, Don accepted the newly created position of Management Development Manager for the Hong Kong Telephone Company. After five years in Hong Kong, where he established the human resource development/organization development function, he returned to the U.S. to serve as professor of human resource development for Marymount University in Arlington, Virginia. He is currently adjunct professor in the Graduate School of Business at Marymount University and at Curtin University in Perth, Western Australia. Don holds a BSAE from Purdue University and masters and doctorate degrees in human resource development from George Washington University.

Alex Douds has over 25 years of experience in human and organizational performance consulting. As Director of the Performance Skills Group, a Division of Human Technology, Inc., he has directed more than 125 performance-improvement projects for private and public-sector clients, with special emphasis on programs in the design and implementation of "best practice" human resource management processes and learning systems, leadership development programs, team performance systems, workforce productivity, and competency-based performance improvement interventions. His most recent works include *The Complete Guide to Managing Change and Transition*, and *Teams: How to Build a Team-Based Organization*, both published through HRD Press in 1998. Alex's private-sector client list includes General Dynamics, Bell Atlantic, H.B. Fuller, Air Products and Chemicals, Inc., Blue Cross and Blue Shield, Genzyme, AGFA, and Ford Motor Company. Public-sector clients include the National Imagery and Mapping Agency, Defense Systems Information Agency, Federal Aviation Administration, U.S. Department of Justice, and the U.S. Department of Health and Human Services.

Module 1
Introduction

Contents

The Need for Consulting Skills 1-1
Consultant Competencies 1-1
Workshop Objectives 1-3
Workshop Plan 1-3

The Need for Consulting Skills

Customer focus... Partnering... Quality... Responding to Changing Markets... Taking Advantage of Technology... Continuous Improvement... Teamwork...

These are some of the strategies today's organizations are embracing in order to successfully compete in the current business environment. And they are turning to consultants, both internal and external, to help guide them in the selection and implementation of strategies specific to their business requirements.

The nature of staff support is also changing. In the past, staff representatives functioned predominantly as the experts, telling their organizational counterparts what to do and what not to do. Today, staff people are being asked to operate in a more consultative role, partnering with their clients to help them anticipate and avoid problems and assisting them in achieving their organizational goals.

Consultant Competencies

Certain general competencies are associated with the consulting role. These competencies are shown on the next page. You can use this list to assess the skills and knowledge you currently have, and to prioritize your learning needs based on the requirements of *your* particular consulting role.

Consultant Competencies

Competencies	Skills and Knowledge Required
1. Marketing	Assessing organizations for consulting opportunities; initiating marketing contacts; promoting services.
2. Contracting	Clarifying client objectives; establishing clear contractual arrangements.
3. Data Gathering	Selecting appropriate data-gathering methods and samples; designing data-collection protocols; administering data-collection processes.
4. Data Analysis	Using appropriate data-analysis methods; maintaining objectivity during analysis.
5. Change Implementation	Determining readiness for change; identifying points of potential resistance; developing change strategies; helping the organization adapt to change.
6. Project Management	Accurately assessing needed resources; meeting time and resource commitments; modifying approaches to achieve project requirements.
7. Problem Resolution	Identifying and resolving roadblocks to goal achievement; dealing with sensitive or unpopular issues; maintaining an advocacy for project goals.
8. Interpersonal Influence	Establishing sound client relationships; understanding others' perspectives; working effectively with diverse people; maintaining credibility and influence with all.
9. Team Facilitation	Incorporating group-development and group-dynamics principles into operating methods; using strategies that promote team productivity.
10. Communication	Listening for understanding of various issues and perspectives; reacting effectively to others' perspectives; communicating articulately, persuasively, and at the appropriate level for the audience.
11. Professionalism	Staying current; using sound/proven processes; operating within professional and legal ethics; maintaining objectivity; recognizing own motives, limitations, and biases; maintaining professionalism under stressful conditions.

Workshop Objectives

This workshop is designed to provide the processes and procedures you need to function most effectively as a consultant.

This workshop includes sound consulting models you can follow and time-tested tools you can use in your consulting. You will find that these models and tools will not only increase your effectiveness as a consultant, but that they will also enhance your professionalism in your clients' eyes.

Successful consulting requires the ability to build and maintain strong relationships with your client and with others in the client's organization. This workshop will pay special attention to how to develop and use the interpersonal skills necessary to build and maintain relationships throughout the consulting process.

By the end of this workshop, you will be able to . . .

- Use systematic consulting processes in performing your role as a consultant.

- Build client credibility and maintain strong client relationships throughout the consulting process.

Workshop Plan

This two-day workshop is divided into eight training modules. The topics included in each of the eight modules are shown below.

Day	Module	Contents
1	1	**INTRODUCTION** ❖ Welcome and introductions ❖ General requirements of consulting ❖ Workshop overview ❖ Participants' expectations
	2	**GENERAL CONSULTING CONCEPTS** ❖ Mini case study ❖ Consulting Fundamentals ❖ Peter Block's Flawless Consulting Process
	3	**PHASE I: ENTRY AND CONTRACTING** ❖ Exploration meetings ❖ Exploration meeting role play ❖ Contracting
	4	**PHASE II: DATA COLLECTION AND DIAGNOSIS** ❖ Interviews ❖ Interviewing exercise ❖ Focus groups ❖ Focus group role plays
2	4	**PHASE II: DATA COLLECTION AND DIAGNOSIS (continued)** ❖ Data analysis ❖ Data analysis exercise
	5	**PHASE III: FEEDBACK AND THE DECISION TO ACT** ❖ Feedback principles ❖ Presenting feedback data to the client ❖ Feedback meeting exercise
	6	**PHASE IV: IMPLEMENTATION** ❖ Resistance to change ❖ William Bridges' Transitions Model ❖ Implementation case study
	7	**PHASE V: EXTENSION, RECYCLE, AND TERMINATION** ❖ Evaluating consulting projects ❖ Evaluation exercise ❖ Tips on the final consulting phase
	8	**CLOSING ACTIVITIES** ❖ Summary of learning ❖ Workshop evaluation

Module 2
General Consulting Concepts

Contents

Introduction 2-1
Module Objectives 2-1
Key Points of the Module 2-2
Exercise 2-1: Falcon Travel 2-3
Flawless Consulting 2-5
Checklists 2-8

Introduction

In this module you will become familiar with the fundamentals of successful consulting. A brief case study will help illuminate these fundamentals.

This module will also define and clarify consulting terms, the kinds of skills consultants must have, and the consulting roles people can play.

The consulting model used as a framework for this workshop was developed by Peter Block and first described in his book, *Flawless Consulting*. You will review the five phases of Block's model and the important tasks associated with each phase. Also included will be four key principles that lead to "flawless consulting."

Module Objectives

By the end of this module, you will be able to . . .

- Describe the general principles involved in effective consulting.

- Describe a five-phase consulting model and the consulting tasks associated with that model.

- Describe the principles involved in "flawless consulting."

Key Points of the Module

- A consulting opportunity starts with a business problem—a "gap" between what is and what should be. You and the client work in partnership to solve the problem.

- Peter Block's five-phase consulting model provides a road map for you to use in performing your consulting role.

- Flawless consulting requires partnering, developing commitment for change, acting authentically, and trusting yourself.

Exercise 2-1:
Falcon Travel

When the Vice President of Staff Operations of Falcon Travel read Rockford's brochure, she started to pitch it into the wastebasket. But something made her stop and look at it more closely. Rockford Consulting's specialty was helping organizations improve their financial results, just what the CEO of Falcon Travel had been harping about in her weekly staff meetings for over two months now. To her knowledge, Falcon Travel had never before engaged a consulting firm to help with its problems, but maybe it was time for just such a move. She picked up the phone and gave Rockford Consulting a call.

The two consultants sent by Rockford Consulting were impressive. They were impeccably dressed and handled themselves professionally throughout the meeting. But what sold Falcon Travel's vice president was a slide show that included graphs of the financial improvement other organizations had realized by hiring Rockford Consulting. When the time came for Falcon Travel's CEO to approve the consulting contract, the vice president had no trouble getting it signed, particularly when the CEO saw that the contract included a money-back guarantee if Falcon Travel's financial results could not be improved by at least 10%.

Once the contract was signed, the Rockford consultants asked the vice president to supply organization charts showing the various operations of the company and the number of people employed in each operation. She was promised a schedule of the consulting reviews and lead time so that she could notify her operations managers about the pending reviews. True to their word, Rockford sent the schedule. The vice president quickly faxed a letter to each operations manager explaining the consulting project and asking for their help in providing the consultants with the information they needed.

The consultants began their reviews within a few days. That was when the calls from the operations managers started to come in. Some of the operations managers had not read the fax. Others had seen it, but still didn't understand what the study was about. All were upset about the situation. "Who are these people?" "What are they going to do with the information?" Falcon's employees were even more upset about the "surprise" intrusion by the consultants, as they expressed it. Some refused to answer the consultants' questions; others threatened to walk off the job if the situation continued.

It took a few days for the vice president to deal with the commotion, but eventually all of Falcon Travel's employees were able to continue performing their jobs under the watchful eyes of the Rockford consultants. However, as one Falcon Travel employee later explained, "Each time I had to tell a customer sitting across my desk why this stranger with a notebook was watching us, my blood boiled."

Finally, the review process was completed. The Rockford consultants left the premises, promising to be back with their consulting solutions. When they returned, they met with the CEO and vice president to present their recommendations. Their report recommended significant changes to Falcon Travel's business operations, and explained that a 15% improvement in their financial results, mostly through force reductions, would be realized if the changes were made. The consultants left an invoice for their consulting service and packed up their materials, pleased to add another client "success story" to their slide show.

The CEO directed the vice president to implement the recommendations as soon as possible in order to quickly gain the benefit of the cost reductions.

When the vice president met with her operations managers to discuss the recommendations, two key operations managers resigned on the spot. Both were upset about the way in which the consulting project was conducted and the anticipated demoralizing effects the outcome would have on their staffs.

The vice president and the remaining operations managers developed a plan to implement the recommendations. When the plan was presented to the employees, resentment and hostility ensued. A number of employees left Falcon Travel to seek employment elsewhere. The majority of those who remained resisted the changes. In some instances, planned implementations failed and had to be rescinded. Some changes were faulty in their concept; others lacked necessary workforce support to make them successful. In one case, an employee was fired because he complained about the situation to a customer, who then wrote a letter to the CEO defending the employee's views.

Ultimately, the vice president resigned.

Despite the internal upheaval caused by the way the process was handled and the failure of many implementation recommendations, Rockford Consulting touted its "successful" work for Falcon Travel in its marketing literature and sales pitches to prospective clients.

Discuss as a group:

1. What went wrong?

2. What should have happened instead?

Flawless Consulting

Consulting Terms

Consultant — A person in a position to have some influence over an individual, a group, or an organization, but who has *no direct power* to make changes or implement programs. A manager is someone who has direct control over the action. The moment you take direct control, you are acting as a manager.

Client — A single individual, a work group, a department, or a whole organization. The client is the person or persons whom you want to influence, without exercising direct control.

Intervention — The goal or end product in any consulting activity: a training program, a new compensation package, a new software program, a new safety program, etc. A planned action in response to an identified need.

Types of Skills Required of Consultants

Technical Skills — Specific skills in an area of expertise (engineering, sales, human resource development, accounting, software engineering, etc.) that you possess, and that the client has need for.

Interpersonal Skills — The ability to put ideas into words, to listen, to give support, to disagree reasonably, to maintain a relationship.

Consulting Skills — Competency in the execution of the tasks underlying the consulting process.

Consultant Roles

Expert — As a consultant, you present yourself as the expert. When called on to solve a problem, you examine the situation, decide what needs to be done, and direct the corrective action. The client plays an inactive role during the consulting process, judging and evaluating after the fact.

Pair-of-Hands — The client knows what needs to be done, but does not have the time or the wherewithal to deal with the problem. As a consultant, you play a passive role during the process.

Collaborative   You enter the relationship with the client with the understanding that your specialized knowledge as well as the client's knowledge of the organization are each required to solve the problem. Problem solving becomes a joint undertaking. The client is actively involved throughout the consulting process.

The Consulting Process

Phase I. Entry and Contracting

Phase I includes the initial contacts with the client about the project. It includes the first meeting, during which you and the client explore the problem, whether you are the right person to work on this issue, and how you should proceed. This phase culminates in the establishment of a contract, fully agreed upon by both you and the client, that clearly defines the nature of the project, its scope, and the mutual expectations of the client and you.

Phase II. Data Collection and Diagnosis

As a part of the contract, a data collection plan, responsive to the client's problem and the nature of the organization, is developed. This phase involves you implementing that plan by doing such things as designing questionnaires, conducting interviews or focus groups, observing operations, and so forth. To the extent possible, both you and those in the client organization are involved in the data collection and the analysis of the data.

Phase III. Feedback and the Decision to Act

The data and analysis are presented to the client for consideration, decision, and action planning. Your role includes presenting the data in a way that ensures that resistance to the data is minimal and the number of issues is manageable, and that the client has viable alternatives to consider. You facilitate the decision-making process so that decisions lead to action plans, with specific assignments and accountability built in.

Phase IV. Implementation

This phase involves carrying out the plan of the previous phase. You may or may not be involved in the actual implementation. For large change efforts, the consultant often helps design and conduct educational sessions about the change.

Phase V. Extension, Recycle, or Termination

This phase begins with an evaluation of the implementation. Following this, the decision is made as to whether to extend the process to other segments of the organization or to tackle new problems. If no further consultative work is required, you conclude the consulting relationship in a professional manner.

Flawless Consulting Principles

Partnering with Clients

Enter the relationship with the client on a 50-50 basis. You and the client share responsibility for the project and each of you has his or her own role to play in arriving at a successful solution.

Developing Commitment

The consultant, by definition, has no direct control over implementation. The client and his or her organization must implement the change. Involving the client and the organization throughout the consulting process is key to developing commitment to the change.

Acting Authentically

This is the most powerful thing that you can do to have the leverage you are looking for and to build client commitment. Client trust is perhaps the most valuable commodity a consultant can obtain. It is developed through honesty in what you do and in what you say.

Trusting Yourself and Your Experience

The contract confirms that the client believes that you have the needed expertise and skills to be a partner in solving the client's problem. You have the technical, interpersonal, and consulting skills necessary to perform your role. Rely on those skills and your past experiences, and trust your instincts to make the right decisions in difficult situations.

Adapted from *Flawless Consulting: A Guide to Getting Your Expertise Used*, by Peter Block.

Checklist #1
Assessing the Balance of Responsibility

	Client Has Major Responsibility, I Have Little	50/50	I Have Major Responsibility, Client Has Little
1. Defining the Initial Problem	←		→
2. Deciding to Proceed with the Project	←		→
3. Selecting Dimensions to Be Studied	←		→
4. Who Is Involved in the Study?	←		→
5. Selecting the Method	←		→
6. Data Collection	←		→
7. Funneling the Data	←		→
8. Data Summary	←		→
9. Data Analysis	←		→
10. Feedback of Results	←		→
11. Recommendations	←		→
12. Decision on Actions	←		→

Connect the marks you made. Any place the line deviates from the center shows an opportunity for you to restructure this project, or your next one, and take full advantage of client involvement to increase your chances of success—especially the chances that your project will still be active and used after you have left the scene.

From: *Flawless Consulting: A Guide to Getting Your Expertise Used*, by Peter Block.

Checklist #2
Analyzing One of Your Contracts

Pick a complicated contract that you have negotiated. Write up the elements of that contract, using the following headings:

1. The Boundaries of Your Analysis
2. Objectives of the Project
3. The Kind of Information You Seek
4. Your Role in the Project
5. The Product You Will Deliver
6. What Support and Involvement You Need from the Client
7. Time Schedule
8. Confidentiality
9. Feedback to You, Later

From: *Flawless Consulting: A Guide to Getting Your Expertise Used*, by Peter Block.

Checklist #3
Planning a Contracting Meeting

1. What imbalance do you anticipate in the responsibility of this project? Do you think the client will want to treat you as the expert and give you 80% of the responsibility? Or will the client treat you as a pair-of-hands and keep 80% of the responsibility?

2. What do you want from the client?

   - What are your *essential* wants?

   - What are your *desirable* wants?

3. What are you offering the client?

   - Technically?

   - Personally?

4. What do you think the client might want? List all possibilities.

   - Technically?

   - Personally?

Checklist #3 (continued)

5. Are the key clients going to be in the room?

    - Who can make a decision on proceeding with this project?

    - Who will be strongly affected by this project?

    - Who is missing from the meeting? What are their roles? (For example, get some action on the problem started, actually implement the outcome of your consultation; they have the best information on the problem.)

6. What resistance do you anticipate?

7. What are the conditions under which it would be best not to proceed?

From: *Flawless Consulting: A Guide to Getting Your Expertise Used*, by Peter Block.

Checklist #4
Reviewing the Contracting Meeting

1. How would you rate:

	CLIENT		CONSULTANT
• Balance of participation?	100%_____	50/50	_____100%
• Who initiated?	100%_____	50/50	_____100%
• Who had control?	100%_____	50/50	_____100%

2. What resistance or reservation did the client express?

   • Which did you explore directly, in words, with the client?

   • Which did you not really explore?

3. What reservations do you have about the contract?

   • Which did you put into words with the client?

   • Which did you express indirectly or not at all?

4. How did you give support to the client?

Checklist #4 (continued)

5. How did the client's concerns get expressed?

    - ☐ Silence?
    - ☐ Compliance?
    - ☐ Attack?
    - ☐ Questions?
    - ☐ Giving answers?
    - ☐ Directly in words?

6. What facial and body language did you observe?

7. How would you rate the client's motivation to proceed?

8. How would you rate your own motivation to proceed?

9. What didn't you express to the client?

10. What would you do differently next time?

From: *Flawless Consulting: A Guide to Getting Your Expertise Used*, by Peter Block.

Checklist #5
Planning a Data-Collection Meeting

To prepare for a data-collection meeting, here are some guidelines to consider. They cover the business of the data collection, and also help you prepare for any resistance you might encounter.

1. Asking questions is an *active* intervention. Use the meeting as an opportunity to deal with resistance and generate interest and commitment.

2. The response you get provides valuable data on the ultimate implementation of your expertise. Notice how the client manages the discussion with you:

   - How much interest and energy is there on this project?
   - On which points is the client uneasy or defensive?
   - On which points is the client open to learning and change?
   - Where is the client unrealistic in estimating the ease or difficulty of some action?

3. What is your understanding of the present problem? Now, based on your experience, what do you think your layers of analysis will yield?

   Layer 1: What technical/business problems is the client likely experiencing?
   Layer 2: What other factors might be contributing to the problem? Who are the other likely actors in the problem?
   Layer 3: What is the client doing that is helping create the problem or preventing it (unknowingly) from being solved?

4. What organizational folklore, history, and culture surrounds this project? Who are the ogres and angels in the client's setting? Accepting folklore as truth is part of what blocks resolution. Identify potential blind spots.

5. You can support and confront during the meeting.

   - What support can you give the client at this point? (Examples of observations you can make: not getting good data; client is over-answering questions and controlling discussion too much; client is omitting key discussion areas; client is answering questions with one-word answers; client is allowing constant interruptions in the meetings; client is skipping around too much; client doesn't believe in project or is playing down seriousness or implications of the problem; client has negative attitudes about consultants in general.)

6. What nonverbal data can you look for? What kind of message does the setting of the meeting convey about client commitment and involvement in your project?

7. What data do you want to collect about how the organization is functioning?

From: *Flawless Consulting: A Guide to Getting Your Experience Used*, by Peter Block.

Checklist #6
Reviewing the Data-Collection Meeting

Your notes contain the content of the data collection meeting. Here are some questions to answer afterward about the process of the meeting. It also is a review of the concepts involved in a data-collection effort.

1. How did the client manage the discussion?

   Client Control　　　　　　　　　　　　　　　　　　　　　**Consultant Control**
   100%　　　　　　　　　　　　　　　　　　　　　　　　　　　　**100%**
   |—————————————————————————————————|

   No Client Energy　　　　　　　　　　　　　　　　　　　　　**Very High**
   for the Project　　　　　　　　　　　　　　　　　　　　　**Client Energy**
   |—————————————————————————————————|

2. What is the technical problem?

3. What other factors are contributing to the problem?

4. What is the client doing to create the problem or prevent its resolution?

5. What folklore, history, ogres, and angels can you identify on this project? Any blind spots the client is missing?

6. What support statements did you make?

Checklist #6 (continued)

7. What confronting statements did you make?

8. What nonverbal clues did you pick up?

From: *Flawless Consulting: A Guide to Getting Your Experience Used*, by Peter Block.

Checklist #7
Planning a Feedback Meeting

Here are some guidelines you can use to help you prepare for a feedback meeting.

1. What do you want from the meeting? Understanding? Agreement? Action? Further work?

2. Structure the meeting so you have at least as much time for discussion as for presentation of results.

3. Review the wording of any feedback to make it as nonevaluative and descriptive as possible.

4. Which elements of your message are likely to generate defensiveness by the client?

5. What form is the defensiveness or resistance likely to take?

6. What questions can you ask to get the resistance *expressed* in the meeting?

7. Who might be missing from the feedback meeting who has a high stake in the outcome?

8. How can you ask for feedback on how this consultation is going?

From: *Flawless Consulting: A Guide to Getting Your Experience Used*, by Peter Block.

Checklist #8
Reviewing the Feedback Meeting

Here are some questions to ask yourself after a feedback meeting. Answering these questions should help you to assess your own learning from each feedback meeting you conduct and to prepare for the next one.

1. What was the outcome?

2. What was the final understanding of the problem or solutions? Was this different than your initial statement of results or recommendations?

3. What form did the resistance take?

4. How did you respond to the resistance?

    - Take it personally?

    - Give more explanation and data?

    - Seek underlying concerns about control and vulnerability?

5. Did you get stuck at any point?

6. What nonverbal messages did you notice?

7. What connections can you make between the way the feedback meeting was managed and the way the technical/business problem is being managed?

Checklist #8 (continued)

8. What effect on your relationship with the client did this meeting have?

9. What would you do differently next time?

From: *Flawless Consulting: A Guide to Getting Your Experience Used*, by Peter Block.

Module 3
Entry and Contracting

Contents

Introduction	3-1
Module Objectives	3-1
Key Points of the Module	3-2
Exploration Meeting Guide	3-3
Exercise 3-1: Exploration Meeting	3-4
Contract Elements	3-7
Contracting Meeting Guide	3-8

Introduction

In this module you will explore the entry and contracting phase of consulting, the first phase of the consulting model. It will begin with a discussion of the primary sources of consulting projects.

This module will also describe the three steps that make up the entry/contracting process:

1. The initial contact with the potential client.
2. The exploration of the client's problem and how you might help as a consultant.
3. The development and negotiation of the consulting contract.

During this module, you will have a chance to participate in a role play exercise that simulates an exploration meeting with a potential client. Finally, the module will include a discussion of the contracting process, including the important elements that are documented in a consulting contract.

Module Objectives

By the end of this module, you will be able to . . .

- Conduct an exploratory meeting with a client.
- Contract with a client about a consulting project.

Key Points of the Module

- The entry/contracting phase is a critical consulting project phase. When you complete it appropriately, the project is off to a good start.

- The meeting with a client is an opportunity to learn more about the problem as the client sees it, and to begin formulating consulting strategies for solving it. The relationship you develop with your client is enhanced by an organized, efficient exploration meeting.

- The project begins to really take shape once you have defined, in writing, your ideas about it. You and the client must openly express your ideas and reactions to proposed project steps and discuss how you will work together to accomplish those steps.

Exploration Meeting Guide

STEPS	NOTES
1. Begin/enhance the consulting relationship	Demonstrate your eagerness to help the client achieve organizational goals. Express a positive "personal acknowledgement" of your feelings about this meeting or the consulting opportunity.
2. Scope the project.	Get the client's view of the problem/opportunity. Ask what's been done so far; what happened. Help the client clarify the desired future state, when the problem is solved or the opportunity is realized.
3. Explore the consulting help needed.	Get the client's view of how you can help. Suggest project help you are prepared to give, including specific ideas for the project.
4. Identify resources required and any known constraints.	Discuss the parameters of the project. Suggest ideas that involve using resources within the client's organization. Identify preferred data-collection methodology. Find out who will be involved in the decision-making process.
5. Agree on next steps.	Clarify what you and the client will do next: you will develop a proposed project plan, client will gather information and resources needed, etc. Set date for contract review.

Exercise 3-1: Exploration Meeting
Role Play Situation

This role play situation takes place at Cellusat, a large telecommunications company headquartered on the East Coast. Cellusat's core business is the manufacture and sale of satellite-powered cellular phones. Its targeted customers are individual consumers and small businesses.

The prospective client, who will be played by the trainer, is Cellusat's Vice President of Customer Services. Customer Services is a key organizational component. Its employees are responsible for expanding Cellusat's customer base because they are who potential customers call to inquire about Cellusat's products and services. Customer Services employees are also key to ensuring that the corporation retains customers on a long-term basis. They do this by the professional way in which they respond to existing customers when they call in with questions or concerns.

The vice president of Customer Services has contacted Cellusat's human resources department and asked for consulting help from the internal consulting group. The vice president is relatively new to Cellusat, but even in this short time, the vice president has gained a reputation as being "people-oriented" and open to new ways of doing things.

Two internal consultants have been assigned to deal with this request, neither of whom has spoken directly with the vice president as yet. Neither has worked with this particular vice president before, but both are looking forward to the opportunity to do so.

The nature of the problem, as relayed to the internal consultants, is that Customer Services is having significant difficulty attracting and retaining qualified representatives. The vice president knows that the current situation is bad. Internal reports show that the competition is seriously threatening Cellusat's customer base, simply because there are not enough Customer Services representatives available to handle the telephone calls received from current and potential customers.

An exploration meeting has been scheduled for the consultants to meet with the vice president in order to gain more information about the problem and explore ways in which the consultants might help.

When the role play begins, the time is 10:00 a.m. on a Monday morning. The consultants are seated in a conference room reserved by the vice president for this meeting. The vice president will enter, and the meeting will begin.

Exercise 3-1: Exploration Meeting
Exploration Meeting Observation Form

Instructions

Silently observe the consultants, noting specifically what the consultant(s) say and do during each of the steps shown below.

Exploration Meeting Steps

1. Begins/enhances the consulting relationship.

    - Demonstrates eagerness to help.
    - Expresses a positive "personal acknowledgement" to the client.

    _____
    _____
    _____

2. Scopes the problem.

    - Gets the client's view of the problem or opportunity.
    - Asks what's been done so far; what happened.
    - Helps the client clarify the desired future state.

    _____
    _____
    _____

3. Explores the consulting help needed.

    - Gets client's view of how consultants can help.
    - Suggests possible help the consultants can give.

    _____
    _____
    _____

4. Identifies constraints, resources, parameters.

    - Builds toward client system involvement.
    - Identifies data collection methodology preferences.
    - Finds out who will be involved in the decision making.

    _____
    _____
    _____

Exercise 3-1 (continued)

5. Agrees on next steps.

    - Clarifies what the consultants and the client will do next.
    - Sets contracting meeting date.

    _____
    _____
    _____

What did you *especially like* about what the consultants did?

What *suggestions* do you have for the consultants?

Contract Elements

Background

Define the initial problem/opportunity (in terms that will not create resistance by the reader).

Project Goals

Specify the project goals/results, based on expectations discussed in the exploration meeting.

Suggested Project Approach

Specify the suggested approach, including data-collection methods to be used.

Explain review and feedback processes.

Articulate your policy on confidentiality and anonymity of data.

Schedule

Include a tentative project schedule.

Roles

Define the client's role/responsibilities (as you see it).

Define your role and responsibilities.

Evaluation

Point out the need to develop an appropriate process for measuring project success.

Next Steps

Specify what you and the client will do next.

Contracting Meeting Guide

STEPS	NOTES
1. Renew the consulting relationship.	"Check-in" with the client. For example: "How have things been going?" "What has happened since our last discussion?" "How is your day going so far?"
2. Review plan in depth.	Be sensitive to client's needs, preferences. For example: "Do you want time to read it over first?" "Do you want to read and ask questions as you go?" "Shall I walk you through it?"
3. Discuss concerns.	Ask for client's concerns. Express own concerns, if any.
4. Modify plan elements.	Focus on collaboration. - Clarify that it is only a draft. - Encourage the client to suggest changes.
5. Clarify next steps.	Clarify what you and the client will do next.
6. Assess the consulting process so far.	Ask for the client's feedback. Give own views. Include supportive comments that reinforce the client's participation and collaboration.

Module 4
Data Collection and Diagnosis

Contents

Introduction 4-1

Module Objectives 4-2

Key Points of the Module 4-2

Comparison of Data Collection Methods 4-3

One-to-One Interviews 4-4

Exercise 4-1: Interviewing 4-7

Focus Groups 4-9

Exercise 4-2: Practice Focus Group 4-13

Creating Questionnaires 4-15

Data Analysis 4-17

Exercise 4-3: Data Analysis 4-19

Introduction

This module deals with the second phase of the consulting model: Data Collection and Diagnosis. The module includes three data-collection methods commonly used to collect data about a client's problem. Those methods are one-to-one interviewing, focus groups, and questionnaires. During the data-collection segment of the module, you will have a chance to experience a one-to-one interview simulation, and you will participate in a practice focus group that will collect data on a common issue faced by most organizations at one time or another.

The module also deals with the diagnosis of the client's problem. You will practice organizing and analyzing data, using the raw data collected in the practice focus-group session.

Module Objectives

By the end of this module, you will be able to . . .

- Conduct a one-to-one interview.
- Run a focus group.
- Describe how to develop and administer questionnaires.
- Analyze data collected about a client's problem.

Key Points of the Module

- The data-collection and diagnosis phase of the consulting process provides the critical data the client will ultimately use to make decisions for improving the organization.
- There are a variety of data-collection methods to choose from. Each should be considered for its effectiveness in developing the quantity and quality of data necessary to solve the problem.
- The data analysis process requires the use of a framework to organize and objectively review the data. Potential areas for change are developed based on the data. Findings that appear to be significant to solving the problem are included, as are unanticipated issues uncovered during the data-collection process that were significant to the respondents.

Comparison of Data-Collection Methods

METHOD	ADVANTAGES	DISADVANTAGES
Interviews	*Adaptive*—allows branching to subjects of importance to interviewee. *Source of "rich" data*—probing enables in-depth understanding. *Empathic*—process of interviewing can build rapport.	Can be expensive. Interviewer can bias responses. Coding/interpretation problems can occur when comparing data across interviews.
Questionnaires	Responses can be quantified and easily summarized. Enables data collection from large samples. Relatively inexpensive.	Nonempathic. Predetermined questions may miss issues. Data may be overinterpreted or meaning misinterpreted.
Focus Groups	Relatively fast and inexpensive. Stimulates idea generation among participants. Allows for in-depth probing.	May be difficult to get group together at one time. A few participants may influence the group. Participants may be reluctant to express views publicly.
Observations	Collects data on behavior rather than reports of behavior. Real-time, not retrospective. Removes respondent bias.	Costly. Samples may not include important/usable data. Coding/interpretation problems can occur when comparing data across samples.

One-to-One Interviews

Preparation Requirements

Preparation for a successful one-to-one interview involves preparation of the interviewer, the interviewee, and the environment.

The interviewer must think through the issues that need to be explored, and then prepare an interview guide about the questions that will elicit reliable data about those issues. The collaborative consultant asks the client to review the interview guide, making adjustments as appropriate. There may be questions overlooked, or questions the client feels are not appropriate for his or her organization.

The interviewee must also be prepared for the interview. He or she needs to be assured in advance that the activity is legitimate—that it is part of a problem-solving process important to the organization, and that it is sanctioned by the organization's leadership. The interviewee also needs time to think about the issues before being interviewed.

The environment must also be properly prepared. An appropriate location for the interview must be selected. It should be comfortable, private, and quiet, and allow for uninterrupted discussion. The choice of location should communicate to the interviewee the importance of the interview and the interviewee's importance in providing data about a significant organizational problem. All documents, writing instruments, reference materials, etc., needed to facilitate the interview should be available at the interview location.

Interviewing Skills

Establishing and Maintaining Rapport

A primary goal of the interviewer is to make the interviewee feel as comfortable with the interview process, and with the interviewer, as possible. The interviewer begins the rapport-building process by openly welcoming the interviewee and making statements designed to set the interviewee at ease. These statements include:

- An introduction of the interviewer, if not known by the interviewee.
- Why the interview is being conducted.
- How the interview will proceed.

Interviewing Skills (continued)

- Assurance that the interviewee's data will be handled on an anonymous basis, with no attribution of comments made to him or her as an individual.

- The importance of the interviewee's data to the solution of the organizational problem.

Throughout the interview, the interviewer demonstrates that he or she is paying close attention to and is respectful of the interviewee's responses.

Questioning Efficiently

The interviewer uses both "open" and "closed" questions throughout the interview process. Open questions, those requiring more than a "yes" or "no" answer, encourage the interviewee to be expansive in his or her answers. Closed questions, on the other hand, tend to limit answers. The interviewer chooses the appropriate form of question, taking into account the contradictory needs of both speed and accuracy.

When the interviewee is not responsive to questions, the client may need to restate the question or clarify the intent of the question. Care should be taken not to "lead" the interviewee or to influence the direction of his or her answers. Interviewer statements are merely to keep the interview on track and to facilitate accurate answers.

Listening and Observing

The first step in listening is paying attention. The interviewer demonstrates this by leaning forward a bit, which also tends to sharpen the senses. Paying attention also includes maintaining eye contact to the degree possible while taking notes, and encouraging the interviewee by smiling, nodding, and so forth. By paying attention to the interviewee, the interviewer can detect the feelings of the interviewee, which are important in understanding the interviewee's perspective.

The interviewer's body language can be perceived by the interviewee as either supporting or contradicting his or her words. The interviewer needs to be aware of his or her own body position, gestures, etc., to ensure that the messages being sent are encouraging ones from the interviewee's perspective.

Interviewing Skills (continued)

Note-Taking and Summaries

The interviewer must take careful notes during the interview to allow for accurate summarization and analysis after the interview. Periodically during the interview, and always at the end, the interviewer should read back to the interviewee a summary of his or her notes and get the interviewee's feedback on their accuracy.

Exercise 4-1: Interviewing

The purpose of this exercise is to provide you with practice in interviewing.

You will pair up with another participant in the class for this practice. One of you will be the interviewer and the other will be the interviewee. You will decide which role each of you will play.

The person playing the **interviewee** will talk about a problem he or she has. It does not need to be a work problem—it can be any problem in real life that the interviewee is experiencing and wants to solve. For example, it might be something like trying to housebreak a pet or deciding whether or not to replace your roof.

The person playing the **interviewer** will ask questions about the problem and practice applying the interviewing skills we've been discussing in the workshop. The interviewer should *not* offer solutions to the problem during the interview. The questions for the interviewer to ask are shown on the next page. The interviewer should take notes during the interview and feed back the summary to the interviewee at the end of the interview.

Exercise 4-1: Interviewing
Interview Questions

1. What is the problem?

2. What have you tried so far?
   - What was the result?

3. What else have you tried?
   - What was the result?

4. What other solutions could you try?
   - What do you think would happen if you tried some of those solutions?

5. How do you want to proceed with the problem now?
   - What do you want to do first?

Focus Groups

Focus Group Characteristics

A focus group meeting generally lasts from one to two hours. Going beyond that time becomes counterproductive. Participants become weary after that time, as they would in any type of data-collection setting.

An effective focus group consists of eight to twelve people. Fewer than eight persons might not provide the range of ideas needed to gain full insight into the problem. More than twelve people, however, might not allow enough time for all participants to express their views freely.

Focus group members are picked for their particular knowledge or experience with the topic, or because they share similar characteristics, such as the length of time they have been in the organization, their job levels, and so forth. While participants share common characteristics, it is from their varying views that a true picture of the problem and its solutions can be discerned.

Participants must freely express their views if the goal of the focus group is to be met. The facilitator is responsible for asking questions that stimulate conversation within the group, yet keeping the discussion moving toward the data collection goals. The facilitator is also responsible for maintaining a nonthreatening and nonevaluative climate that encourages free expression of participants' views.

Focus Group Steps

1. ***Discuss the focus group with the client.***

    You and the client must clarify the logistics: the date the meeting is to be held, the timing, location, number of participants, refreshments to be served, and so forth.

    The participants should also be discussed and selected. The goal is to select the appropriate combination of people for discussing the problem. Combinations that might restrict data flow, such as bosses and subordinates, might not make the atmosphere conducive to free and open discussion of the issues.

    The client's role must be clarified. For example, the client needs to make sure that participants are informed in advance of the time and location for the meeting, its importance, and the intended use of the data. It is also helpful for the client to "kick off" the focus group, welcoming participants, stating the

Focus Group Steps (continued)

purpose of the data-collection effort, and emphasizing the anonymous nature of the data. However, it is not appropriate for the client to be present during the actual discussion of the issues by the focus group.

You should also discuss with the client the importance of giving feedback to the focus group members after they have provided their data. While all organization members should be kept informed of the status of a significant problem-solving effort, those who participate in focus groups have a heightened desire to know how their contributions were received and used.

2. Draft a focus-group guide.

There are three components of a focus-group guide:

1) An introductory section, which includes welcoming the participants and conducting introductions. (An "icebreaker" is also helpful at this point.) Participants are told the reason for the focus group, why they were chosen as focus group members, and how the focus group will proceed. It is also useful to display a list of ground rules for the meeting, such as:

   - All points of view are encouraged and accepted.
   - Silence is OK.
   - Only one person is to speak at a time.
   - Disagreement is OK, but no personal attacks.
   - Confidentiality will be maintained.

2) A section that lists the questions the facilitator will ask during the focus group meeting. The guide often includes helpful notes for the facilitator to use during the session, such as areas marked for specific probes or indications when consensus-testing may be appropriate.

3) A closing section that includes asking participants for their final comments, expressing appreciation for their time and their data, and explaining the next steps that will be taken in relation to the data. If the client intends to provide feedback to the participants about their data or the project in general, this information is passed on to the group at this time.

3. Review the guide with the client.

Review the interview guide with the client, and make modifications to the agenda or to the questions, as needed.

Focus Group Facilitator Tasks

1. Conduct introductory activities.

The facilitator conducts introductions, starting with himself or herself, in a way that helps put the group at ease. For example, introductions are often combined with icebreakers, such as having people include a "fun fact" about themselves (a hobby, a recent vacation, etc.) as each introduces himself or herself.

The facilitator clarifies the purpose and objectives of the focus group meeting, providing background on the problem being investigated and how the meeting will help.

The facilitator states the ground rules for the meeting, emphasizing the confidentiality requirements associated with participants' providing information about the problem. The facilitator assures participants that while their views will be summarized, individual identities will be protected. The facilitator (and others on the consultant's team) and all focus group members must be bound by confidentiality guarantees regarding data that is generated in the meeting.

2. Facilitate discussion of the issues.

The facilitator follows the focus-group guide, modifying it as appropriate during the session.

The facilitator encourages the group's participation by asking open-ended questions, which stimulate conversation and discussion among participants. The facilitator also uses body gestures that encourage participants, such as walking toward them, smiling, nodding, and so forth. The facilitator draws out persons who are quiet by asking, in a nonthreatening way, their opinions about the subject being discussed.

The facilitator listens, elicits elaboration, and moves the discussion along while allowing participants a chance to be heard on the issues. When necessary, the facilitator reminds participants of the ground rules for the meeting.

The facilitator limits his or her own statements and avoids any comments that might appear to provide "the answer."

Focus Group Facilitator Tasks (continued)

The facilitator tests for consensus, when needed, to provide clarity as to the strength of particular viewpoints and to move the discussion along. If there isn't consensus, the facilitator asks why, in order to more fully explore viewpoints. If consensus cannot be reached, the facilitator polls the group so that the numbers of people on each side of the issue can be included in the final report.

3. **Summarize the issues discussed.**

   The facilitator reviews the discussion to assure participants that they have been understood. This step also ties the information together in a logical manner and provides a sense of closure to all participants. The facilitator should ask participants for any final comments they might have before closing the meeting.

4. **Close the meeting.**

   The facilitator thanks the group for their attendance and their contributions.

   The facilitator explains what will happen with the data from this point, and how the client will provide feedback to them, if the client has agreed to this step.

Exercise 4-2: Practice Focus Group

This exercise is intended to provide practice with focus group methodology. It will give you a feel for the roles of the facilitator, recorder, and focus group member.

We will return to the problem situation described in the Cellusat case, which we began to explore during Module 3. At this point, the client and the consultant have determined that a focus group would be appropriate for collecting data about the organization's problem—how the organization can attract and retain high quality employees. A focus group of current employees has been selected to provide data on that problem.

The class will be divided into two groups:

- Participants in one group will each play the role of a focus group member. You will find that the topic of the focus group discussion is one that people in any organization can provide input about. It is important that focus group members play their roles as realistically as possible. If you are a member of this practice focus group, **provide input as though you were considering this problem from your own organization's perspective**—how your organization might improve in attracting and retaining high quality employees.

- Participants in the other subgroup will each play the role of a member of the consulting team—the focus group facilitator and recorder roles. You will be given time to identify the individuals who will play:

    - The facilitator—the person who will ask the questions and facilitate the group discussion.

    - The flip chart recorder—the person who will record on the flip chart the data generated from the focus group.

    - A note-taking recorder—a person from the consultant team who takes notes on the group discussion while seated in the back of the room.

    The questions to be asked during the focus-group practice have already been developed and agreed to by the client. There is an overall question that relates to the business problem and four questions to use in probing for solutions to the business problem. These questions are shown on the next page.

When you begin the focus-group practice, assume that the introductory activities have already occurred—the focus-group members have introduced themselves, the reasons for the focus group have been described, and the ground rules have been reviewed. Now is the time for the facilitator to ask questions to get the focus group's input on the client's problem.

Exercise 4-2: Practice Focus Group
(continued)

The overall question that relates to the business problem:

"What does it take to attract and retain high-quality people in our organization?"

Four questions to use in probing for solutions to the business problem:

1. What is our organization doing now that has a positive effect on the problem and needs to be **continued**?

2. What is our organization doing now that has a negative effect on the problem and needs to be **changed** in some way?

3. What is our organization doing now that should be **stopped**?

4. What does our organization need to **start** doing?

Creating Questionnaires

STEP	NOTES
1. Determine what you need to know.	Focus on the project goals.
2. Choose a response format.	**Consider:** Checklists Yes/no answers Multiple-choice questions Ranked or scaled items Fill-in responses Open-ended questions
3. Write the questions.	**Good:** Simple, clear, short, logically ordered, inviting, not too many **Not Good:** Too many, ambiguous, leading, too predictably patterned, boring
4. Prepare a summary sheet.	Consider how you will compile the data when responses are received.
5. Pilot test/revise the questionnaire.	Have testers from the target population take the questionnaire. Have them note unclear wording, other concerns. Review their feedback. Investigate too many "don't know," "blank," or "wrong" answers.
6. Develop introduction.	**Include:** Who commissioned the study Why it is important How responses will be used How to complete/return the questionnaire Assurance that responses will be handled in a confidential manner

Factors in Choosing a Data-Collection Method

FACTOR	CONSIDERATIONS
Data to be collected	What is the nature of the data to be collected?
	Is it sensitive data best obtained through one-to-one interviews?
	Might there be any benefit in individuals hearing and thinking about others' responses?
	Can data be easily obtained by questionnaire without the need to interpret answers?
Resources	What are the resource capabilities and limitations?
	Are respondents located over a wide territory or are there so many respondents that a questionnaire appears to be the most feasible approach?
Organizational preferences	Is the organization inclined to use one method over the other?
	Has the organization overused one method so that its potential for high-quality data collection has been compromised?
Own preferences	If all factors are equal in their potential for effective data collection, does the consultant have a preference for one data collection method over another?

Data Analysis

Data Analysis Frameworks

During data analysis, you must organize the data into a framework that enables interpretation of the data and understanding of its meaning. The framework may be one you prepare before collecting the data, such as summary sheets used to summarize questionnaire information or a framework such as the PIPE model shown below, which can be used to organize the data.

THE "PIPE" MODEL

Procedures	Data related to the organization's policies or procedures
Information	Data related to the organization's information systems or its communication processes
People	Data related to the ways in which the organization manages its employees
Equipment	Data related to the equipment, facilities, tools, or supplies maintained by the organization

Frameworks used to organize and analyze data often emerge from the data itself. These frameworks are the obvious "themes" that can be seen when reviewing raw data.

Regardless of the framework used, it is important to also organize the examples and verbatim comments you noted during the data-collection process. These details become powerful support for consulting recommendations presented to the client for consideration.

Potential Areas for Change

During the analysis of the data, you must sort through it to identify potential areas for change. These are areas that obviously relate to the client's problem and appear to be significant to resolving the problem.

There may be other potential areas for change not directly related to the client's problem. They may deserve consideration, however, due to the frequency with which the issue was reported by respondents, or the extent of emotion respondents displayed when talking about the issue.

Use your judgment when identifying potential areas for change. Clients should be presented with key issues so that their decision making can be focused on the highest potential payoffs to their organization. There may well be issues uncovered during the data analysis process that do not meet the test of significance. In those cases, the data is not reported as a potential change area, and most often is not fed back to the client. However, you may want to include that data in a minor section of the feedback report, or in an appendix.

Exercise 4-3: Data Analysis

The purpose of this exercise is to give you an opportunity to practice organizing data and determining potential areas for change.

You will be working in groups to complete this exercise. The data you will be analyzing is the data collected during the focus group that you participated in earlier in this workshop.

When you are in your group, analyze the data.

- Review and make sure your group understands the data from the first focus group question: "What is our organization doing now that has a positive effect on the problem, and needs to be **continued**?" Then put that data aside for the time being. (You will return to this data in the next exercise.)

- Review and make sure your group understands the data from the remaining three focus group questions. As you review the data, identify the main "themes" that emerge from the data. These will be the broad categories you will use in organizing the data. Cross-reference the data items from the source information (the recorder's notes from the focus group) to the theme categories you identified. Retain the source information: you may need to refer to it in a later exercise.

- Make a note of any items your group needs to clarify further when you return to the total group.

Select a spokesperson to report your group's themes to the total group.

Module 5
Feedback and the Decision to Act

Contents

Introduction 5-1

Module Objectives 5-1

Key Points of the Module 5-2

Criteria for Effective Organizational Feedback 5-3

Data-Presentation Meeting Model 5-4

A Typical Consulting Report 5-5

Exercise 5-1: Feedback Meeting 5-6

Introduction

This module deals with the third phase of Peter Block's consulting model—Feedback and the Decision to Act.

In this module you will consider the principles involved in feeding back organizational data to the client. You will be introduced to the connection between feedback and organizational energy, and you will consider ways to prevent or minimize resistance to feedback.

You will also be given seven criteria that can help you choose and present effective organizational feedback. And you will learn how to structure feedback meetings and present feedback in ways that promote organizational change.

As a final part of this module, you will practice delivering organizational feedback in a meeting setting, and you will participate in a role play simulating that feedback meeting.

Module Objectives

By the end of this module, you will be able to . . .

- Identify key elements involved in providing organizational feedback.
- Plan for a data feedback meeting.
- Deliver feedback effectively.

Key Points of the Module

- Effective feedback creates positive organizational energy, a requirement for organizational change.

- As a part of the collaborative process, you should meet with the client in advance of delivering feedback to the client's organization to discuss the feedback and the meeting agenda. This step enables the client to adequately prepare himself or herself for the meeting, and it results in greater "buy-in" by the client.

- Feedback recipients need time to understand and react to the data during a feedback meeting. An important aspect of your role is to facilitate their understanding and to make sure that all points of view are considered before decisions about the data are reached.

- The feedback meeting should end with a set of action steps agreed upon by meeting participants, based on the feedback data. You should facilitate the action-planning process after delivering the feedback.

Criteria for Effective Organizational Feedback

Use the seven criteria below to increase the effectiveness of the organizational feedback you provide to your clients.

1. **Is it relevant?**

   Is the feedback related to issues that are meaningful to the recipients?

2. **Is it understandable?**

   Are the form, language, and symbols you are using familiar and understandable to the recipients?

3. **Is it descriptive?**

   Have you included real examples and illustrative details based on information developed during the data-collection process? Have you portrayed the respondents' strong feelings about issues?

4. **Is it limited?**

   Have you avoided information overload by excluding less-important data, or at least relegating it to the appendix of your written report?

5. **Is it impactable?**

   Are the feedback issues under the control or influence of the recipients?

6. **Is it comparative?**

   Where possible, have you included data that can serve as comparison points or benchmarks that recipients can use in evaluating the data?

7. **Is it unfinalized?**

   Have you pointed toward more in-depth data-collection possibilities, or ways that others in the organization can be involved in identifying and solving problems?

From *Feedback and Organization Development: Using Data-Based Methods*, by David A. Nadler.

Data-Presentation Meeting Model

Below is a model of the structure and process for a one-hour data presentation meeting.

If your presentation is to a client group, have the client introduce your presentation and reaffirm his or her support for the effort.

STEPS	% Meeting Time	Minutes
1. Restate the original contract, clarifying the problem or goal to be addressed.	5%	3
2. State the agenda and structure for the meeting.		
3. Review project methodology (briefly). Present findings, recommendations. Allow questions for clarification during the presentation.	15%	9
4. Ask for recipients' reactions to the data.	30%	18
5. Check to see if the meeting is going ok.	10%	6
6. Facilitate decision making, action planning.	30%	18
• Decisions on priorities, what to be worked on first.		
• Action items, the "what, who, when" for each.		
7. Test for client control and commitment.	10%	6
8. Ask, *"Did you get what you needed?"*		
9. Offer your services in relation to the implementation and other consulting needs.		
10. Express support in relation to the project and future efforts.		
	100%	60 minutes

Leave a written report.

A Typical Consulting Report

Executive Summary

A brief summary of the project's goals, methodology, findings, and recommendations.

Introduction and Overview

Information about the project and its goals. An overview of the contents of the subsequent report.

Methodology

A description of the data-collection methodology used, sufficient to answer questions of data credibility, but not so extensive as to bog down the reader.

Findings

The major issues related to the project goals, as identified by the data-collection effort.

Recommendations

Recommendations for resolving the issues and problems identified in "Findings."

Appendices

Examples of items included in an appendix are shown below.

- Contract (or project plan or letter of agreement)
- Data-collection tools employed
- Data summaries not included in "Findings"
- Other relevant data or resources supporting the report that are not included in the body of the report

Appendixed items should be referenced at the appropriate location within the body of the report, based on the subject matter involved.

Exercise 5-1: Feedback Meeting

The purpose of this exercise is to give you an opportunity to practice preparing for a client feedback meeting, and to participate in a role play of a feedback meeting.

You will begin this exercise by returning to the group you were working with during the data-analysis exercise in the last module. Your group will now prepare to feed back the data you analyzed during that previous exercise.

To help you with this task, refer to the "Data Presentation Meeting Model" shown in the *Coursebook* on page 5-4. However, because of the time constraints in this workshop, your group will complete **Steps 1 through 4 only**. Your total presentation time for accomplishing these steps will be limited to **30 minutes.**

Also consider the "Criteria for Effective Organizational Feedback" on page 5-3 as you review and organize your feedback data.

Plan to present the positive data that the focus group members provided. (See Focus Group Question 1: *"What is the organization doing now that has a positive effect on the problem?"* etc.). Also plan for presenting priorities for change. These will come from the themes you developed from the focus group data.

Assume that your feedback recipients will include the top management of an organization and his or her direct reporting leadership team.

When you have finished your planning activities, select someone from your subgroup to role play the consultant presenting the data in the feedback meeting with the client and his or her leadership team.

Module 6
Implementation

Contents

Introduction 6-1

Module Objectives 6-1

Key Points of the Module 6-2

Helping People through Change 6-3

Exercise 6-1: Implementation Case—A Case for Change 6-6

Introduction

This module deals with the fourth phase of Peter Block's consulting model—Implementation.

In this module, you will consider implementation from the perspective of the people in the organization who will undergo the organizational changes. William Bridges' work in clarifying how to help people through change will serve as the framework for this module.

As a final part of this module, you will review a case situation involving an organization having serious difficulty implementing a change. You will be asked to select strategies you would recommend to the client to get the implementation back on track.

Module Objectives

By the end of this module, you will be able to . . .

- Identify the key elements required for implementing change successfully.

- Identify actions that help support people through the change process.

Key Points of the Module

- Resistance to change is a natural part of the change process. It stems from feelings of loss that people have when they are faced with major changes in their work environment.

- William Bridges' framework for viewing change from the perspective of those required to make psychological transitions to the change can be a helpful framework for consultants and the leaders of organizations.

- Bridges' framework highlights the need for organizational leaders to be sensitive to people and their needs, *throughout the entire implementation phase*. Two-way communication, empathy, and involvement of people in the change process are essential elements in implementing change smoothly and successfully.

Helping People through Change

"It isn't the changes that do you in, it's the transitions. Change is not the same as transition. **Change** *is situational; the new site, the new boss, the new team roles, the new policy.* **Transition** *is the psychological process people go through to come to terms with the new situation. Change is external; transition is internal."*
　　　　　　　　　　William Bridges

The Transition Process

While not everyone may feel the same way about a particular organizational change, most people go through a similar process when dealing with change. This process is called *transition*.

There are three phases of the transition process: *Endings, The Neutral Zone,* and *Beginnings.* These phases of transition are often not clear or distinct. They tend to overlap. In fact, it is not unusual for people to have feelings associated with all three phases at the same time.

The change or shift in the external environment can happen quickly. The inward psychological transition that people go through, however, happens more slowly. People have to "try out" the change for awhile—see how it feels. Then they can begin to psychologically embrace it.

People progress through the phases of transition at different rates, and individuals vary in their reactions to change. Often, organization leaders are ahead of their employees since they typically know about the change before their employees do, have a clearer vision of where the organization is headed, and have a plan for getting there.

Endings

When people become aware that the change is going to take place, the *Endings* phase starts. The "old way" is coming to an end; people must let go of the past.

During organizational change, people's greatest fears relate to the possibility of losing something of value. These perceived losses are over such things as:

- Personal affiliations and attachments
- Status or position
- Job security
- Familiar ways of operating
- Power and control
- Confidence in themselves or their future

Endings (continued)

To facilitate people through the *Endings* phase, organizational leaders should provide forums for two-way communication about the change. E-mail, memos, and slick publications are not, by themselves, the answer. People need to hear, in person, the "straight scoop" about the change and be encouraged to ask their questions and express their concerns without fear of reprisal. The absence of dialogue at the early point of a change increases feelings of vulnerability and makes it more difficult for people to progress through the *Endings* phase.

People can put the past behind them more readily by "marking the ending." This is something concrete that acknowledges the value of the "old" as the organization goes to the "new." Some examples are farewell parties, memory books, plaques, and pictures.

The Neutral Zone

This is the heart of the transition process. People have begun to let go of the old, but they have not yet accepted the new. It is a time for trying out the change.

The *Neutral Zone* is characterized by ambiguity, loss of identity, and confusion. Work is often at a standstill because people aren't sure about what to do or how to do it. Rumors about the change are rampant, particularly if information is limited, and people aren't sure what the outcome of the change will really be.

Temporary systems may be necessary to maintain a sense of normalcy and control, and to facilitate getting the work done. People need to feel that systems are either in place or will be put in place so that the change will work right.

If things don't go well in the *Neutral Zone*, people become discouraged and often try to revert back to old methods and behaviors. This is the time to solicit views from people about how the change is going. Timely adjustments to the implementation based on people's input can make the change go more smoothly, for the organization and for its members.

Trust in the organization's leadership is crucial during this phase. Frequent two-way communication about the change helps build this trust.

Beginnings

When people are finally ready to psychologically commit to the new way, they have entered the *Beginnings* phase. They begin to incorporate new understandings, values, and behaviors called for by the change. They show signs of investment in the change, identifying with the new way, rather than with the old.

Beginnings (continued)

The acceptance of the change and its requirements results in people wanting to modify their behavior to make the change work. They look for concrete evidence of their success. Organizational leaders need to provide encouragement, support, and reinforcement during the early parts of this phase, even if some mistakes occur.

Celebrations marking the achievement of significant change goals or milestones solidify commitment to the change. A "victory party" or a tee shirt can go a long way in saying "thank you" for helping make a change successful.

Participation and Communication

When people are involved in the change, it is "our change," not "their change." Involvement should begin at the beginning—during the data collection activities that lead to the change recommendation—and continue throughout the implementation process.

Two-way communication is critical for early acceptance of change. Organization leaders can use the "4P's" as a guide:

- **P**urpose: Why the organization is changing.

- **P**icture: What the outcome will look like, and how the people will fit into that picture.

- **P**lan: Steps the organization will take to implement the change, including the training and support people need to do their jobs.

- **P**art: The roles of other people in shaping and guiding the change.

Finally, and very importantly, organization leaders help people through their psychological transition to the change by engendering trust. Here are some actions that help build trust:

- Listening.
- Being honest.
- Saying "I don't know " (when you don't).
- Passing along known information.
- Being visible and keeping an "open door."
- Soliciting and responding to people's views and concerns.
- Allowing people to express their emotions.
- Acknowledging that this is a difficult time.
- Showing personal commitment to the change.

Adapted from *Managing Transitions: Making the Most of Change*, by William Bridges.

Exercise 6-1: Implementation Case

The purpose of this exercise is to give you an opportunity to put on your consultant hat and help a client who is having difficulty implementing an organizational change.

You will work on this case study individually. First, read through the details of the case that begins below. Then, follow the instructions at the end of the case to complete the case study.

A Case for Change

A computer software firm did most of its business over the telephone. One of its major employee groups consisted of customer service employees who handled customer questions and responded to customer operating difficulties.

Calls from customers who had purchased software programs from the firm were handled by people at three different levels. First, the calls were routed to relatively inexperienced employees who could answer basic questions. They received the calls on a first-available basis. If the problem was too difficult for them, they tried to get help within their level first. If the problem still couldn't be solved, the call was transferred to the second level of customer service employees.

Customer service employees at the second level had more training and experience and could field most of the calls. If they could not take care of the problem, after talking it over with others in their same level, they passed it on to level three.

Level three customer service employees were programmers totally familiar with the program in question. These employees could, when necessary, teach the customer how to reprogram portions of the software to solve the customer's problem.

The firm's culture was based on strong individualism. The term "individual contributor" was used consistently in describing employees who were meeting their job objectives.

Each customer service level had a manager. Employees were evaluated by their manager primarily on the number of customer calls handled each day. Call volume objectives were established through a manager–employee discussion at the beginning of the evaluation period. If an individual reached his or her objective, he or she received a bonus.

The general manager was not happy with the way the customer service organization was operating.

1. Customers complained about the length of time it took to be transferred from one customer service person to another and the need to re-tell their story.

A Case Study for Change (continued)

2. Coordination between the customer service groups was nil. Sometimes one manager group would "busy out" the entire group to enable the group to "catch up" on their work. This resulted in a higher level of customer dissatisfaction and a higher level of frustrated workers among the other manager groups.

3. Another software firm was vying for their customers and promising that customer service would be their number-one business priority.

To deal with the problems, the general manager asked a consultant to study the situation and recommend solutions. The resulting recommendations were that the organization be restructured into six teams of people from each of the three customer-service groups. Customers would be assigned to a team, which would be given the collective responsibility for solving that customer's problem.

The change was explained at an organizational meeting. At the meeting, the new organization charts and new procedures were presented. The general manager explained the importance of the change and emphasized the importance of each team's part in making the change successful.

Team coordinators were appointed to route the calls to the appropriate resource in their teams. All of the managers became coordinators; the three remaining coordinators were drawn from the customer service employee force. Training for the coordinators and customer service representatives was provided in time for the established "cutover" date to the new way of operating.

When the cutover occurred, there were problems. At first, it was thought that the problems were just typical of a radical change. But after a month, it was clear that the problems weren't going to go away by themselves. In fact, customers were still being tossed back and forth between teams. Coordinators were maintaining their old ties with people from their former teams. They would ask for help from former team members rather than call on new team members they didn't know so well.

On the following pages, there is a list of actions you might take to deal with the situation. Scan them first, then go back through the list and put a number by each item, assigning it one of the following five categories:

1 = Very important. Do this at once.
2 = Worth doing, but takes more time. Start planning it.
3 = Yes and no. Depends on how it's done.
4 = Not very important. May even be a waste of effort.
5 = No! Don't do this.

Possible Actions

1. _____ Explain the changes again in a carefully written memo.

2. _____ Figure out exactly how individuals' behavior and attitudes will have to change to make the teams work.

3. _____ Identify who stands to lose something under the new system.

4. _____ Redesign the compensation system to reward those who comply with the changes.

5. _____ "Sell" the problems that are the basis for the change.

6. _____ Bring in a motivational speaker to give employees a powerful talk about teamwork.

7. _____ Design temporary systems to contain the confusion during the cutover from the old way to the new way.

8. _____ Use the interim between the old system and the new to improve the way in which services are delivered by the organization. Where appropriate, create new services.

9. _____ Put team members in contact with disgruntled clients, either by phone or in person. Let them see the problem firsthand.

10. _____ Appoint a "change manager" to be responsible for seeing that the changes go smoothly.

11. _____ Give everyone a badge with a new "teamwork" logo on it.

12. _____ Break the change into smaller stages. Combine the first and second customer service levels, then add the third level employees later. Change the managers into coordinators last.

13. _____ Talk to individuals. Ask what kinds of problems they have with "teaming."

14. _____ Pull the best people in the unit together as a model team to show everyone else how to do it.

15. _____ Give everyone a training seminar on how to work as a team.

Possible Actions (continued)

16. _____ Reorganize the general manager's staff as a team and change the general manager's job to that of a coordinator.

17. _____ Send team representatives to visit other organizations where service teams operate successfully.

18. _____ Turn the whole thing over to the individual contributors as a group and ask them to come up with a plan to change over to teams.

19. _____ Scrap the plan and find one that is less disruptive.

20. _____ Tell people to stop dragging their feet or they'll face disciplinary action.

21. _____ Give bonuses to the first team that processes 100 customer calls in the new way.

22. _____ Give everyone a copy of the new organization chart.

23. _____ Start holding regular team meetings.

24. _____ Change the annual individual targets to *team* targets, and adjust bonuses to reward *team* performance.

25. _____ Talk about transition and what it does to people. Give coordinators a seminar on how to manage people in transition.

Adapted from *Managing Transitions: Making the Most of Change*, by William Bridges.

Module 7
Extension, Recycle, or Termination

Contents

Introduction 7-1
Module Objectives 7-1
Key Points of the Module 7-1
Evaluation Planning 7-3
Exercise 7-1: Planning an Evaluation 7-6

Introduction

This module presents an overview of how to evaluate consulting projects. It discusses the importance of conducting evaluations and explains the two basic types of evaluations.

You will review a model for developing an evaluation plan, and use that model to practice developing a plan during the module.

Finally, the module will deal with the fifth and final phase of Peter Block's model—Extension, Recycle, or Termination. You will learn what each of these actions entails, including things you *must* consider when a consultant ends his or her involvement with a consulting project.

Module Objectives

By the end of this module, you will be able to . . .

- Develop components of a project evaluation plan.
- Describe the elements involved in the final phase of consulting.

Key Points of the Module

- Develop a preliminary evaluation plan that details what you want to know, what should be measured, the sources and methods of data collection, and the appropriate timing of the evaluation.

- Review the preliminary evaluation plan with the client. Make adjustments based on the client's feedback.

Key Points of the Module (continued)

- Perform the final consulting phase professionally and appropriately. If there are additional problems to solve, or similar problems in other parts of the client's system that need your help, return to Phase I to explore the problems and negotiate a contract for solving them.

- When termination of your services is appropriate, leave in a timely and professional manner. Make sure the client system is equipped to continue without your assistance. Reinforce the positive relationship with your client as you discuss the project and give positive feedback about the client's contributions to the project's success.

Evaluation Planning

When designing an evaluation to measure results of a consulting project, the important question to be answered is, *"Did the organization achieve what it wanted to achieve?"*

There are five key questions to consider in planning for an evaluation to answer that primary question.

1. **What do we want to know?**

    Dr. Donald Kirkpatrick's four-level evaluation model[1] for evaluating training programs can be useful in thinking through this question for consulting projects. For example:

Results Data:	•	Did the change result in the problem being solved?
	•	Are organizational objectives being met?
Reaction Data:	•	Are employees responding well to the change brought about by the project?
	•	Is there strong support for the change at all levels of the organization?
Behavior Data:	•	Have employees changed their behaviors as necessary to support the change?
	•	Is the organizational culture, including its formal and informal policies and procedures, supportive of the change?
Learning Data	•	What has the organization learned from the project that might be helpful in the future?

2. **What should be measured to determine what we want to know?**

    Typical measures include such things as:

    - Measures of customer and employee satisfaction.
    - Measures of quality, quantity, efficiency, and timeliness of products or services.
    - Financial measures, such as sales, profit/loss ratios, revenues, and expense levels.

[1] Kirkpatrick, Donald J., *Evaluating Training Programs: The Four Levels*, 2nd edition, Berrett-Koehler, 1998.

Evaluation Planning (continued)

3. **Where should the data come from, and how should it be collected?**

   Both people and documents should be considered as sources of data.

   Organizational records, such as personnel records and performance or production results, can be helpful in gaining insights into project outcomes.

   People are significant sources of evaluation data. Multiple points of view are important to elicit. Exactly whose views should be heard and how much weight they should have hinges on the organization's culture, value system, overall goals, and what you are trying to measure. For example, if quality improvement of products and services was the problem to be solved, then customers should have the loudest voices in evaluating the results.

   Methods for collecting evaluation data include:

   - Interviews—both one-to-one and group interviews, conducted by telephone or other electronic media, or in person.

   - Survey questionnaires.

   - Observation: watching people perform tasks, examining records, reports, and other available documentation, etc.

   Who collects the data and interprets the results depends on what data are being collected, from whom, and how. Whether to use independent data collectors or members of the organization itself is a decision that must be made by the organization's leadership. In some cases, putting the responsibility of evaluation into the hands of the organization, including those being evaluated, serves to strengthen support for the change that resulted from the consulting effort.

4. **When should we measure?**

   Evaluation timing must be thought through carefully.

   Assessments must not be done prematurely. Sufficient time should elapse in order to get a good reading of the outcomes.

   Delaying too long keeps the organization from making timely necessary adjustments to the implementation of solutions. Delays can also result in complicating the evaluation picture. Organizations are constantly changing, and project evaluations become more difficult to interpret when significant changes have occurred.

Evaluation Planning (continued)

5. What will be done with the results?

Specific questions to ask yourself here are:

- To whom should the results be reported back?

- Who will make decisions based on the evaluation?

- What is the best way to communicate about the evaluation and decisions made as a result of the evaluation?

Exercise 7-1: Planning an Evaluation

You will return to the group you were working with during the feedback meeting exercise, Exercise 5-1.

Assume that the client accepted all of the priorities for change that your group recommended during Exercise 5-1, and that implementation has begun. Now your group will develop a preliminary plan for evaluating the Cellusat consulting project's results.

Use the worksheet on the next page to help you develop your evaluation plan. Plan for answering the first four planning questions as described on pages 7-3 and 7-4 in this section of your *Coursebook*.

When you have finished your planning discussion, select someone from your subgroup to report on your group's plan.

Evaluation Planning Worksheet

1. What do we want to know?	2. What should be measured?	3. Where should the data come from? How should it be collected?	4. When should we measure?

Consulting Skills Workshop
Workshop Evaluation

For each of the areas covered by the workshop, indicate:

- How much you knew about the area **before** the workshop.
- How much you know **now** about the area.
- How valuable you think having the knowledge/skill in the area will be back on the job.

Assign a rating of 0 to 9 for each of the three questions, using the scale below.

0	1 2 3	4 5 6	7 8 9
Nothing/ No Value	Little	Some	A Lot

Knew Before	Know Now	Workshop Area	Value
		General Consulting Concepts • General principles involved in consulting effectively • Peter Block's 5-phase consulting model	
		Entry and Contracting • Conducting an exploration meeting • Documenting a consulting contract	
		Data Collection and Diagnosis • Conducting a one-to-one interview • Running a focus group • Tips in developing and administering questionnaires • Analyzing data collected about a client's problem	
		Feedback and the Decision to Act • Key elements in providing organizational feedback • Planning a data feedback meeting • Delivering feedback effectively	
		Implementation • Key elements in implementing change successfully • Actions that support people through the change process	
		Extension, Recycle, or Termination • Planning for an evaluation of a consulting project • The elements involved in the final phase of consulting	

Workshop Evaluation (continued)

1. Overall, how satisfied were you with the workshop?

0	1 2 3	4 5 6	7 8 9
Very Dissatisfied	**Dissatisfied**	**Satisfied**	**Very Satisfied**

2. How much did the workshop contribute to your professional development?

0	1 2 3	4 5 6	7 8 9
Very Little Contribution	**Little Contribution**	**Some Contribution**	**A Large Contribution**

3. How much did the workshop contribute to your personal learning goals?

0	1 2 3	4 5 6	7 8 9
Very Little Contribution	**Little Contribution**	**Some Contribution**	**A Large Contribution**

4. What training needs do you still have that should be addressed?

Other comments: